Momentous Materials
Silicon

by Dalton Rains

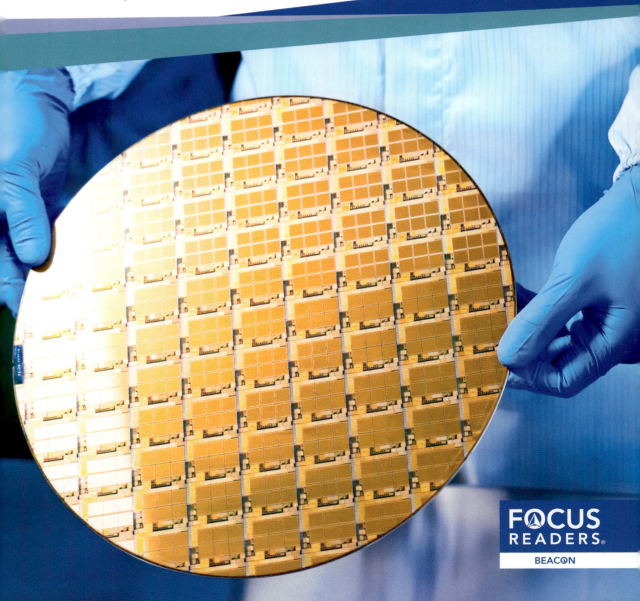

www.focusreaders.com

Copyright © 2024 by Focus Readers®, Mendota Heights, MN 55120. All rights reserved. No part of this book may be reproduced or utilized in any form or by any means without written permission from the publisher.

Focus Readers is distributed by North Star Editions:
sales@northstareditions.com | 888-417-0195

Produced for Focus Readers by Red Line Editorial.

Photographs ©: Shutterstock Images, cover, 1, 8, 13, 14–15, 16, 19, 20, 22, 24, 27, 29; Ulrich Baumgarten/Getty Images, 4; Christian Charisius/dpa/picture alliance/Getty Images, 7; Hulton Archive/Archive Photos/Getty Images, 11

Library of Congress Cataloging-in-Publication Data
Library of Congress Cataloging-in-Publication Data is available on the Library of Congress website.

ISBN
979-8-88998-036-0 (hardcover)
979-8-88998-079-7 (paperback)
979-8-88998-161-9 (ebook pdf)
979-8-88998-122-0 (hosted ebook)

Printed in the United States of America
Mankato, MN
012024

About the Author

Dalton Rains is a writer and editor from Saint Paul, Minnesota.

Table of Contents

CHAPTER 1
Making Microchips 5

CHAPTER 2
History of Silicon 9

THAT'S AMAZING!
Solar Cells 14

CHAPTER 3
How It Works 17

CHAPTER 4
Uses of Silicon 23

Focus on Silicon • 28
Glossary • 30
To Learn More • 31
Index • 32

Chapter 1

Making Microchips

A factory worker turns on a machine. It pours sand into a container. The container gets very hot. The sand melts. Materials in the sand separate. A piece of silicon is left behind.

The tube-shaped piece of silicon is called a boule.

Next, the silicon goes to a second machine. It cuts the silicon into thin **wafers**. Then each wafer goes to another machine. Light shines on certain parts of the wafer. These areas get harder. Light doesn't shine on other parts of the wafer. These areas get **etched** away.

Did You Know?

Most microchips take several months to make.

 Dust can ruin microchips. So, the factories that make microchips are very clean.

The wafer is now a **microchip**. It can be used in a computer. Microchips allow computers to perform tasks. They can also store information. Silicon is a very useful material.

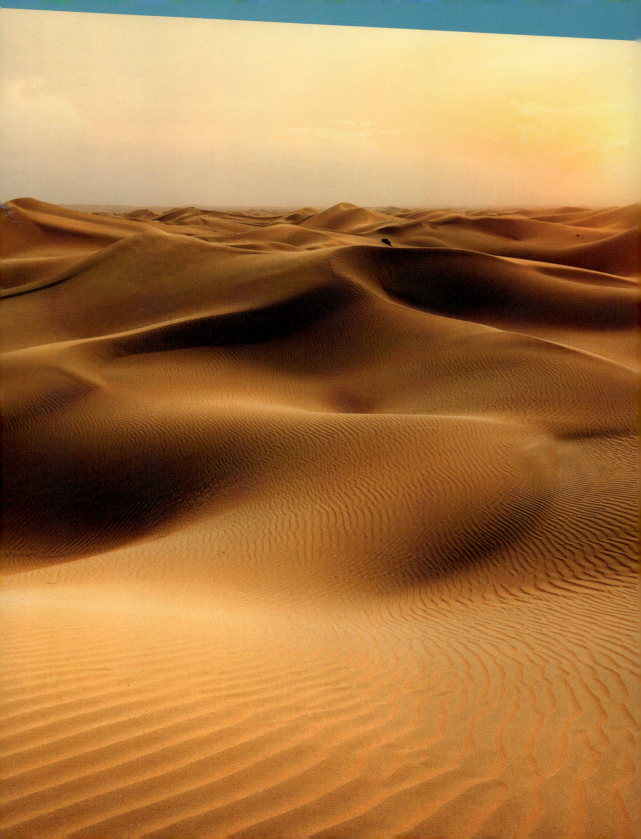

Chapter 2

History of Silicon

Silicon can take many forms. In nature, it is always part of a compound. That means the silicon is blended with other materials. For example, silicon is in sand and clay. It is also in most rocks.

Sand is one of the most common materials on Earth.

People used these materials for thousands of years. They made glass with sand. They made bricks with clay. They built walls with rock. But they did not know how to make pure silicon. That changed in the 1800s. First, scientists heated material with silicon in it. Then they mixed in water. This step helped separate the silicon.

Scientists used pure silicon to create new devices. In 1954, they made the first silicon **transistor**.

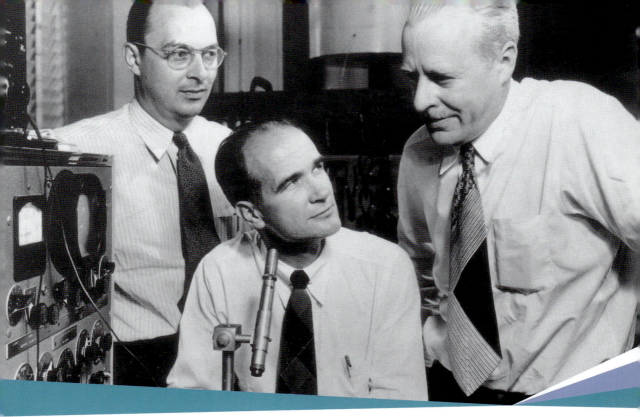

 The scientists who invented transistors won the Nobel Prize for their work.

A transistor can be used in two ways. First, it can work as a switch. It turns an electric **current** on or off. Computers use transistors in this way.

11

A transistor can also work as an **amplifier**. A small current flows through one part. That causes a bigger current to flow through another part. Radios use transistors in this way.

Scientists figured out how to combine many transistors. They

Early computers did not use transistors. These computers were very big. They filled entire rooms.

 Smartphones use billions of tiny transistors.

made devices called microchips. Over time, scientists made smaller and smaller transistors. More could fit on one microchip. Chips could be smaller, too. As a result, computers became faster and smaller.

THAT'S AMAZING!

Solar Cells

In 1940, a scientist was studying silicon. One of his **samples** had a crack in it. When light hit the sample, electricity flowed through it. One side had a positive charge. The other side had a negative charge.

The scientist's work helped people invent **solar cells**. These cells use sunlight to make electricity. When light hits a cell, an electric current starts flowing.

Later, scientists linked several cells together. They formed a solar panel. It produced power. Over time, more and more people started using solar panels.

Today, many homes are powered by solar panels.

Chapter 3

How It Works

Some materials are conductors. Electricity flows through them easily. Copper is one example. It is often used for wires. Other materials are insulators. They block the flow of electricity.

 The wires used in power lines are conductors.

Rubber is an insulator. It is used to cover wires. That stops electricity from shocking people.

Silicon is different. It is a semiconductor. That means electricity can flow through it. But it can also block the flow of electricity.

However, silicon must be altered before it can be used in this way. This step is called doping. Scientists add tiny amounts of other materials. These materials

 A wafer can be made into many microchips.

change part of the silicon's charge. That affects how electricity moves through it. Now it works well for transistors.

 Silicon transistors allow computers to operate very quickly.

After silicon is doped, each transistor can act as a switch. It can be open. This allows electricity to flow. Or it can be closed. This stops electricity from flowing.

In computers, these switches send signals. The signals tell computers what to do. Computers use a language made up of zeroes and ones. An open transistor means zero. A closed transistor means one. Computers use this language to **process** information.

Did You Know?

Computer language is called binary. Computers turn binary into letters. For example, 01010011 is binary for the letter S.

21

Chapter 4

Uses of Silicon

Silicon microchips are key parts of technology. They are in almost all electronic devices. Computers and smartphones use them. So do cars and airplanes. Scientists continue to improve microchips every year.

 Hearing aids use transistors to make things sound louder.

 Pacemakers use transistors. These devices help people with heart problems.

They make the transistors smaller. That helps the chips run faster.

A typical microchip is the size of a fingernail. But the transistors on it are very small. One chip can have billions of transistors.

Machines etch patterns onto microchips. Different kinds of chips have different patterns. There are two main kinds. One kind is a logic chip. Logic chips help process information and complete tasks. They also help with graphics.

For instance, a logic chip might help run a game on a smartphone.

Memory chips are another kind. These chips store information. They can do this even when a device is turned off. For instance, a memory chip might help store photos on a computer.

Did You Know?

Many people put microchips under their pets' skin. That way, lost animals can be returned to their owners.

 Doctors give pets shots to insert small microchips.

Silicon is all around us. It is one of the most important materials on Earth. Without it, many devices would not exist.

FOCUS ON
Silicon

Write your answers on a separate piece of paper.

1. Write a paragraph describing the main ideas of Chapter 2.

2. What do you think is the most interesting way silicon is used? Why?

3. What kind of microchip helps a computer complete tasks?
- **A.** logic chip
- **B.** memory chip
- **C.** solar cell

4. Why might smaller transistors help a computer run faster?
- **A.** The computer can hold more transistors.
- **B.** The computer becomes very hot.
- **C.** The computer does not weigh as much.

5. What does **altered** mean in this book?

*However, silicon must be **altered** before it can be used in this way. This step is called doping. Scientists add tiny amounts of other materials.*

    A. separated
    B. destroyed
    C. changed

6. What does **graphics** mean in this book?

*They also help with **graphics**. For instance, a logic chip might help run a game on a smartphone.*

    A. the pictures people see on a screen
    B. devices people use to make calls
    C. people who are good at video games

Answer key on page 32.

Glossary

amplifier
Something that makes a weak signal stronger.

current
The flow of charged particles.

etched
Removed part of a surface to create a specific shape.

microchip
A small, flat piece of silicon that holds many transistors.

process
To follow a series of steps in order to get an answer.

samples
Small pieces taken from a larger object for study.

solar cells
Devices that turn the sun's energy into electricity.

transistor
A device that controls the flow of electricity by turning on or off.

wafers
Thin, flat objects.

To Learn More

BOOKS

Fromowitz, Lori. *Building a Computer*. Mendota Heights, MN: Focus Readers, 2020.

Kim, Carol. *Hidden Heroes in Technology*. Minneapolis: Lerner Publications, 2023.

Smibert, Angie. *Inside Computers*. Minneapolis: Abdo Publishing, 2019.

NOTE TO EDUCATORS

Visit **www.focusreaders.com** to find lesson plans, activities, links, and other resources related to this title.

Index

A
amplifier, 12

C
clay, 9–10
computers, 7, 11–13, 21, 23, 26
conductors, 17
current, 11–12, 14

D
doping, 18, 20

E
electricity, 11, 14, 17–20
etching, 6, 25

I
insulators, 17–18

L
logic chip, 25–26

M
memory chip, 26
microchips, 6–7, 13, 23, 25–26

R
radios, 12

S
sand, 5, 9–10
semiconductor, 18
solar cells, 14

T
transistors, 10–13, 19–21, 25

W
wafers, 6–7

Answer Key: 1. Answers will vary; **2.** Answers will vary; **3.** A; **4.** A; **5.** C; **6.** A